BLESSED ARE THE MEEK

SON OF SOLOMON ON
EDUCATION, BUSINESS
& SUCCESS.

WILLIAM OKYERE

This book represents a serious effort, time
and resources from the author.

Therefore, no part of this book may be reproduced in any
form or by any means, electronic or mechanical,
including photocopying or recording or by any
information storage and retrieval system without
permission in writing from the publisher.

Faulting these directives is unlawful and unethical.

For details about other books by author and speaking
arrangements please contact him on:
+233 (0) 557 581 505
email: pneumeduf@yahoo.com.

ISBN: 978-9988-0-9174-3

© 2006
Pastor William Okyere

Printed & Published by:
Pastor William Okyere
Tel: +233 (0) 557 581 505
pneumeduf@yahoo.com.

Others by William Okyere

Patience

Time Your Life

Incline Thine Ear

Spiritual Bootcamp

The Prodigal, The Proclamation & The Prophetic

Introduction

The most controversial issues in our part of the world and also among Christians are issues concerning Education, Business & Success.

Many cannot answer questions like: Who is truly educated? Who is a successful person? Does it matter how we attain success? Is success possible to all?

Whiles this book does not attempt to answer these questions, it will provoke the readers thoughts in his attempts to answer them.
 Enjoy it.

William Okyere

1. Education is a lifestyle; it is not a certificate.

2. True education humbles; empty education puffs up.

3. One of the several wonders of the world; the ignorant are rather more difficult to teach.

4. Many hold on to philosophies not because they are good, but because they bought them with hard currency at the university; too expensive to let go.

5. Many identify the educated by the cars they ride in; identify yours by their character.

6. It is more difficult to work with the mind than the physical body. Energy comes by eating the delicious; wisdom comes by thinking through difficulties.

7. It is more painful for those who at the top to fall than those lower down the ladder. He that is down need no fall.

8. The cautious ones lead by management principles. The sacrificial ones lead by example.

9. Is there anything that is important to you? Give it a big name. Invest some money into it as well.

10. Employers seek gain; employees demand appropriate compensation. The situation can be explained in terms of action and reaction; they must be opposite and equal.

11. Many in this life, receive help too late;
    either by having their mortuary fees paid or
    receiving donations from those who only want
    to identify with their success.

12. There is a type of 'food'– those who eat less of it
    are more satisfied than those who eat much –
    Money. You can't have enough of it.

13. When you get obsessed with the fear of losing
    your job, you will surely lose the benefits the job
    is to bring you.

14. Bad business, very often, starts with a bad
    business man.

15. There are still many ways to success, even from
    a poor start.

16. A cent, adding up to ninety-nine others to make one dollar, can be more valuable than a quarter standing alone. Let's harness our resources.

17. Plan for the things you need before your wants drag you into debt.

18. Work, Work, Work, Work, Work, Work,
    Six days thou labor and do all thy work.
    (Exodus 20)Work must be so much important to God to give us six days of seven days to pursue. Please do something positive with your life.

19. There are no better king makers than education, hard work and excellence. Why do you have to wait all your lifetime for some tribal heads to enthrone you as chief? No wonder Ghana is overwhelmed with chieftaincy disputes.

20. Both Skill and money bring wealth. Make sure you have one of them.

21. What we do for business is not necessarily what brings success but how we do them. Excel.

22. Workers are to paid according to the work they do; not according to their needs.

23. Success is very difficult to maintain ;the more you succeed, the harder you must work to maintain it.

24. He that does not respect process will not see progress. Plan.

25. Effectiveness is not measured by how excited performers are about their pursuits; it is measured by time.

26. The space you cover at a particular time determines your speed; not how fast you feel you are running. All can read true achievements.

27. It is not how large you are that determines your impact; it is rather how compact you are. Claim only the 'land' you can cultivate.

28. In life, bigger things are built out of the small; you cannot achieve the big until you identify the small.

29. Important issues will only look important by the ladder of other issue they climb –Prioritize.

30. Aims not pursued act as obstructions to growth.

31. The first step towards meeting our needs is rising- up with the intension to do so.

32. Planning makes you your own supervisor. That is the most efficient way to success.

33. When there are no laid down procedures, there are no effective means to trouble shooting.

34. The basis for effective work is not energy but creativity.

35. Productivity should be measured by how much human energy is exerted but how much of it is saved.

36. Being able to gather resources for a task is an indication that one identifies the dimensions of a task.

37. Work is to improve; it is not to kill. Are you dying because of work?

38. Progress made up of movements and stops. The fact that one is not stopping does not necessarily mean he is progressing. Rest is not a setback.

39. What others own represent their wealth; what others possess represent their debts. It is not only gold that glitters, mirages also do.

40. Apart from salvation, many of life goals are achieved by **work**. It is okay to sweat.

41. If you work for the money you cannot share or enjoy, then you have worked as a slave.

42. When people like their work, the role of the supervisor is only a formality.

43. After getting wealthier, some become wiser, others become more foolish and some others die. Climb well.

44. It is more profitable to invest in people's beginnings than their endings; Better to sponsor your child's education than cater for his wedding expenses.

45. You cannot maintain business success without a growing understanding of the importance of the customer.

46. The progressive has more challenges than the static. The static is familiar with all his problems. The progressive, at every stage, faces more challenges. If you are afraid of challenges, stay where you are.

47. Work is not an exertion of energy; it is an improvement of the situation.

48. Processes must be performable; otherwise they act as obstacles.

49. Do you know why God made seeds smaller than fruits? He did so to encourage initiative.

50. Effective beginnings must be comparatively small. You grow before they grow.

51. Do not take a loan for any project with uncertain outcome. Highest risks must not be pursued on loans.

52. Opportunities do not always come. On several occasions, they have to be created.

53. Improvements in finances does not only come by increased income, but also by a trimmed budget.

54. It is more dignifying to dig than to beg. Those who dig do so with purpose and those who beg do so for a purpose.

55. Pray for your competitors, for they assure you that the world can run without you. Isn't that a relief?

56. Do not always go searching for fruit. Many times, the seed is easier to find.

57. Out of every 'fruit' plant a 'seed'.

58. All things will not prosper at all times. Catch the wind.

59. The fear to start is the only future non-starters have.

60. Many plan their lives according to the settings of the past. The future takes them by surprise.

61. We do not overcome cold by changing the weather but by planting cotton to keep us warm.

62. Knowledge without understanding is swollen-headedness.

63. Looks influence quicker; books influence better. Nice haircuts do not shape the brain; Education does.

64. If you want your stomach to remain filled, fill your mind first.

65. Some go to school to learn; others learn to go to school.

66. Education and ignorance are both expensive. The problem with ignorance is that you cannot budget for it.

67. Many of the principles studied in the classroom were discovered outside the classroom. Education is not classroom-bound.

68. Take your time to listen. Information has different variables and people's choices of these affect the angle from which they communicate. Hasty conclusions can be disastrous.

69. Education increases responsibility; excellent grades should indicate maturity.

70. Communication is not only for information but also for motivation. Is it worth saying it over again even if your audience already knows it.

71. The home is the best school for child development; parents, the best teachers and good example, the best curriculum.

72. When your children are not asking you questions, they are not being less troublesome, they may be asking the wrong person instead. Be careful.

73. True education is the type that stirs up further enquiry. Education has no end.

74. Whatever children begin to ask questions about, their intellects are ready to receive.

75. A poor man is only a needy rich man; and a rich man, a wealthy poor man.

76. The chaos in the beginning of creation that God for an answer. Does the chaos around you have you for an answer?

77. Money appreciates when well spent; it loses value when worshipped.

78. A good Christian is not the one who has received many things from God but rather the one who has received much of him.

79. The greatest blessing in this life is to know who Jesus is.(Matthew 16:18)

80. The heaviest load is not the one placed on the head but the one placed on the mind.

81. It is not only darkness that hinders our vision. crookedness also does. Darkness comes from the devil; Crookedness comes from us.

82. Our minds are the measurements of the intensity of our problems.

83. A smile is beautiful. A frown is only dutiful, if it is upon the wrong thing.

84. Though rules are made for progress, they can be tools for the restriction of progress, if not handled well.

85. Some expensive things are cheaper than the cheap. Cheap things can be very expensive.

86. Power is an appetite. Just tasting it addicts. The safest way to handle power is to share it.

87. We are to solve problems effectively; not necessarily quickly.

88. Everything called 'New' is also called a 'Change'. Open up!

89. So many things can be done, without so many things, in so many ways.

90. In this world, many literary works gain more recognition by quoting from expired sources than quoting from the "inspired source".

91. If the cost of living goes higher, do not increase your expenditure until you have increased your income.

92. Motivation strengthens initiatives. Manipulation creates reaction. Initiatives die hard; Reactions die fast.

93. Time produces the best, but only with the appropriate input.

94. At times, and in some situation, it is faster to walk than to run.

95. You may not have the height man is looking for, but you can have the heart God is looking for.

96. One mystery in life:

    Many are able to manage life with little. They rather fail with much.

97. There are different ways of improving a situation. One is to criticize the bad; the other and the more effective, to appreciate the good.

98. The ideal cannot be fantasized into reality. It must be worked out .

99. Good solutions solve problems; they do not crash before them.

100.   What happens to the poor can happen to the rich. Money is the only defense in the hands of the wise.

101.	Among many wrongs, the right stands out. Do not be afraid to do the right.

102.	If just travelling brings success, all that poor nations will have to do is to exchange locations. A passport with a visa does not guarantee success.

103.	To work is to solve a problem. There is nothing like a problem –free work.

104.	If Jesus were to run a business school, many Christian executives will not attend; for fear he will tell them to give up all to follow Him. How committed are you to Him?

105.	We are not to work to get blessed. We are blessed to work.

106.   The eternal God once began a project. No, you are not too old.(Genesis 1:1).

107.   When is a wiser person instructed by the foolish? When the former is poor and the latter, rich.

108.   Those who think money is all there is to life are easily enslaved.

109.   All the music that has been made through the history of this world, has been composed out of eight notes. We can't complain.

110.   Everything 'white' is not always right. Many things 'black' are whiter.

111.   Some are born to rich parents; others to a richer God.

THE END

9 789998 809174 3